The Action of Subtraction

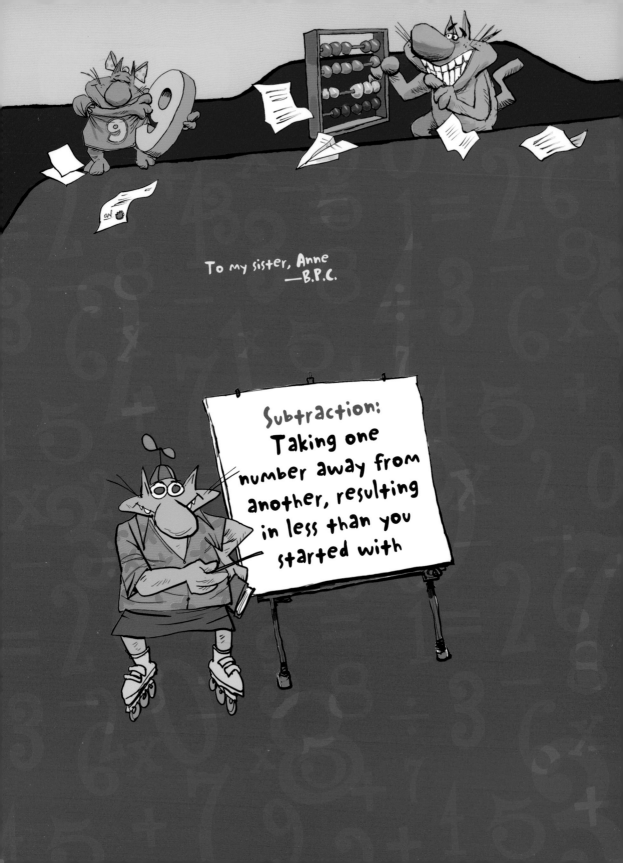

The Action of Subtraction

by Brian P. Cleary

illustrated by Brian Gable

M MILLBROOK PRESS / MINNEAPOLIS

Subtraction is an action that will make your total less,

Whether ice-cream scoops
or hula hoops
or inches from a dress.

Whatever
you are counting,
it will take away a part,

and leave you then
with not as much
as you had at the start.

If 7 angry bulldogs
Were barking at your door,

a kitten could scare **3** away.

Then you'd be left with **4**.

And what if 13 hornets had nested in your tree?

If 10 of them would just buzz off,

you'd then have only 3.

Do you see what **Subtraction** does?

It changes the amount,

So you'll wind up with fewer when you do your final count.

"Minus" means to take away
some number from the whole.

Like if you had
10 bowling pins
and grabbed a ball to roll,

let's say you knocked down 8 pins with the first ball that you threw.

Then 2 would still be standing 'cause

$$\begin{array}{r} 10 \\ \text{minus } \underline{8} \\ \text{is } \quad 2. \end{array}$$

Your second ball knocks
2 more down.

You did it!

You're the hero!

Now all the pins are
down because

$$2$$
minus $$2$$
_____
is $$0.$$

In this case, "is" means "equals,"
or "totals just the same."

That sign means
matching value
in a problem or a game.

Like if you had 3 time-outs left
and somehow lost your shoe,

your coach would have to call 1,
and you'd be left with 2.

3 was what you started with.
Then you Subtracted 1.

That would equal 2 more left
before the game was done.

If Jenn had 12 stuffed animals, and she gave 2 to Sally,

then 5 more
went to Marykate,
here's how you'd do
the tally:

Start with 12. Take 2 away—

$$12 \text{ minus } 2 \text{ is } 10.$$

Subtract the 5 for Marykate.

$$12 - 2 = 10$$

$$10 - 5 = 5$$

Then that leaves 5 for Jenn.

Whenever we **Subtract** things,
it can make us
sad or glad,

depending on
Whatever there
is less of—good or bad.

Like fewer school days
due to snow
and less time with
the dentist,

not as much discomfort since
the doctor fixed your bent wrist.

A smaller plate of vegetables,
a shorter list of chores,
less time with your homework,

and not quite
as many
snores.

See!
The numbers move
toward **0**
with a shrinking
kind of action.

And all of this is possible
because we have Subtraction!

So, what is subtraction?
Do you know?

Find activities, games, and more at
www.brianpcleary.com

ABOUT THE AUTHOR & ILLUSTRATOR

BRIAN P. CLEARY is the author of the best-selling Words Are CATegorical© series as well as the Math Is CATegorical©, Food Is CATegorical©, Adventures in Memory™, and Sounds Like Reading© series. He has also written Six Sheep Sip Thick Shakes: And Other Tricky Tongue Twisters, The Punctuation Station, and several other books. Mr. Cleary lives in Cleveland, Ohio.

BRIAN GABLE is the illustrator of many Words Are CATegorical© books and the Math Is CATegorical© series. Mr. Gable also works as a political cartoonist for the Globe and Mail newspaper in Toronto, Canada.

Text copyright © 2006 by Brian P. Cleary
Illustrations copyright © 2006 by Lerner Publishing Group, Inc.

Millbrook Press
A division of Lerner Publishing Group, Inc.
241 First Avenue North
Minneapolis, MN 55401 USA

For reading levels and more information, look up this title at www.lernerbooks.com.

Library of Congress Cataloging-in-Publication Data

Cleary, Brian P., 1959—
    The action of subtraction / by Brian P. Cleary ; illustrations by Brian Gable.
      p.   cm.
    ISBN 978—0—7613—9461—7 (lib. bdg. : alk. paper)
    ISBN 978—0—8225—7181—0 (eb pdf)
    1. Subtraction—Juvenile literature. 2. Counting-out rhymes—Juvenile literature. I. Gable, Brian, 1949—
ill. II. Title.
    QA115.C54 2006
    513.2'12—dc22   2005025881

Manufactured in the United States of America
12—49594—1063—9/21/2010